MY UNOFFICIAL
─(2nd to last)─
WILL & TESTAMENT

ROBERT
BEIDERMAN

DECORATIONS BY MICHAEL WETSTONE

CONTENTS

For Angelo

Your humor and encouragement
continues to inspire.

FORWARD

"Watch out for that tree!!!"

PERHAPS YOU SHOULD
SIT DOWN FOR THIS

Hello, world.

Or perhaps I should say...
Goodbye, world.

For you see, I am now deceased.
Dead.
Kaput.
Gone.
I kicked the bucket.
I bought the farm.

I'm an emptier vessel than
Lindsay Lohan's parole officer.

As of this moment, you will have to find a way to survive in this world without me.

I wish I could understand the horrible pain you must be suffering through right now, but alas...
I have never had to live in a world without me.

So good luck with that.

Before you try to pick up the
pieces and move on with your now
meaningless life, there is a small
matter of legality.

Attached you will find my
(2nd to last) will and testament.

Please do your best to follow my
wishes to the letter, as it would be
a crime to ignore a dead man's
final requests.

Okay... maybe not a crime, but
let's just say it's frowned upon
here in the afterlife. Already, Martin
Luther King, Jr. and Sonny Bono
are sternly shaking their heads at
the thought of you not following
through on your responsibilities.

Besides, you will find that my wishes are rather simple and painless.

Sure, it will set you back a pretty penny, and you might have to relocate to Beirut for a while.

But it will all be worth the sacrifice of your first born child when you see the smile on my face.

(You will need to pay the mortician a little extra to pinch the corners of my mouth upward.)

SPREADING NEWS
OF MY DEATH

My family and loved ones should
be notified by seeing-eye dogs,
who will bark the sad news in
some form of canine Morse code
in exchange for bacon.

The gossip shall quickly spread
like a forest fire on Facebook,
with some of my more distraught
friends attaching to their
devastating status updates a photo
of a monkey covering his eyes.

I'm not sure how Twitter works,
but I believe the hash-tag,
#goodbyehairynipples
will trend highly for a few weeks.

My good friend, Brian, shall change my voicemail greeting for uninformed callers, complete with directions to the nearest liquor store and instructions on how to overdose on pills.

Just in case you're thinking about joining me in the afterlife.

You don't have to actually go through with it.

Just think about it.

Co-workers will probably notice a black cloth covering my portrait in the ladies' restroom.

Grief counselors should be made available after a staff meeting in which our managing partner shows the entire office a PowerPoint presentation that ends with a photo of my cold, lifeless corpse.

NBC News shall interrupt its
most popular sit-com with a
special announcement, mildly
inconveniencing the 15 people who
are currently watching their most
popular sit-com at that time.

A breaking news update
mentioning my passing
shall appear on both the running
tickers for CNN and ESPN News.

FOX News will most likely declare
that I am alive and well.

My cute upstairs neighbor, Sara,
will probably act like she is having
trouble remembering who I am.

That's just how Sara normally acts
when she's full of grief.

Like a coy, cock-teasing bitch.

I suspect that my Uncle Larry
will shed some tears over this
devestating news.

But if he doesn't, I suppose he can
use a couple of saline drops.

If he still doesn't cry, tie him to a
chair and make him watch the last
hour of *Million Dollar Baby*.

See how Mr. Stoneface reacts to
throwing a puppy in front of a bus.

If all else fails to elicit some
measure of remorse, you may
inform my Uncle Larry that the
salad bar at Sizzler is now closed.

I don't care if people have trouble
seeing chalk outlines in the snow
(or if it's not winter). All great
deaths get a chalk outline.

Classes at Northeastern University
shall be cancelled. In their place
the school should hold an interfaith
vigil, where trustees will point out to
the entire student body that:

    A) I was awesome;

    B) I was taken too soon; and

    C) I did not attend this college.

While I don't expect the
President of the United States
to mention me in his daily press
conference...

(although it would be nice)

I'm sure the Attorney General will
be able to spare a sentence or two,
preferably about those charges
finally being dropped.

To reach some of the more remote locations around the globe, a carrier pigeon shall be dispatched with a heartbreaking note stuffed inside a fortune cookie that is affixed to its beak, along with someone's lucky lotto numbers:

4, 19, 22, -8, 3.14 & Z.

It will fly for thousands of miles, across the Atlantic and Indian Oceans.

Upon reaching Africa, the pigeon
will stop for a brief moment to rest
its wings and be eaten by a zebra.

The zebra will then run across the
length of the entire continent,
before being eaten by a lion.

Weeks later, the lion will be caught
by trappers and sold on Craigslist
for $250, a carton of Camel Lights,
and a pair of cowboy boots that
once belonged to Tom Wopat.

A year later, the lion will be rescued
in a highly complicated and
controversial, international
lion-trapper sting operation and
taken in by the San Diego Zoo,
where after a thorough inspection
the fortune cookie will be found—
still intact, next to an old tire—
and eaten by a very hungry and
underpaid vet.

Not a veterinarian, but a vet who
has just returned home from the
Middle East.

The vet will toss away the note
without reading it.

A month will pass, and a weary family of tourists will pass by the panda exhibit, where a gentle pacific breeze has carried this tragic note of my demise.

Although the husband's eyes are still weary after a long night of arguing over his wife's refusal to attempt that "position" she had promised to try in exchange for a nice vacation, he will notice the discarded note while making a feeble effort to glance up the skirt of a passing nun.

The man (let's call him, Skip)
will find great sadness in this
sobering news, zip up his fly,
and stuff the note in his pocket.

After a long flight home and a
couple of weeks of calm, Skip
will one day return home to find
his clothes and other possessions
scattered about on the front lawn.

Apparently, someone found his
secret stash of seagull beaks.

Before Skip can collect all of his belongings, a local vagrant will snatch the pair of pants with the note in its pocket and wander off to a back alley, where he can celebrate his new riches with a giant bottle of peach schnapps.

A couple of hours later, after urinating on a police car, the vagrant will be strip-searched by a pack of angry DJ's during a live radio broadcast for charity.

The DJ's will find the note and read this horrible news on the air.

And that's how the fine folks of Birmingham, Alabama will learn about my death.

PREPARING MY BODY

My freshly-deceased body is to be
washed thoroughly by members
of the United States field hockey
team in a tub made of solid silver,
filled with 300 bottles of Aquafina.

I am to be air-dried on a bed of
rose petals, which will then be
made into perfume for the field
hockey team to wear during their
next Olympic-qualifying match.

When they win that match,
it shall be in my honor.

Losing is not an option.

Once properly dry, Sergei, my
personal barber from Queens,
is to be permitted entrance.

Sergei will probably act as if he's
never met me before and might
wonder why he's being forced at
gunpoint into my chambers.

Don't be alarmed; that's just how
Sergei acts when his wife and kids
are being held hostage.

Under careful watch, Sergei is to
shave my back-hairs, which will
then be donated to cancer patients.

Just because they are undergoing
chemotherapy, doesn't mean they
shouldn't also go through the
same embarrassing nuisance of
unwanted hairs as the rest of us.

I am to be posthumously fed a final meal consisting of filet minion and whipped sweet potatoes, by local missionaries from Jews for Jesus.

They shall take turns placing the food into my mouth and gently rocking my jawbone back and forth in a chewing motion, while softly singing religious hymns in my right ear.

For dessert I will allow myself a slice of sugar-free pumpkin pie, or something else that doesn't make me feel too bloated.

My organs are to be
donated to needy people...

(Aside from that one
kidney which we'll sell
on the black market to
pay for my funeral)

So that these people will
owe me big time once we
all get to heaven.

It will be worth the wait
to get an extra half cloud
to float on and a second
harp to string.

My blood is to be extracted and
used to paint a duplication of
Starry Night, by either:

A) a direct descendent of
   Vincent Van Gogh; or

B) anyone else named Vincent.

It shall tour museums around the
world, until it takes part in our first
mission to Mars as an example
to the Martians of how rational
Earthlings function.

My embalming fluid shall be made entirely out of Kettle One vodka.

All my life, friends teased me for not being able to hold my liquor, but look who's laughing now, punks!

Most importantly, and before <u>any</u> of these activities take place...

I am to be removed from that necrophilia club I joined last year.

THE FUNERAL

Dressed in my finest leisure suit,
my body shall lie in repose at my
summer home in Hooker Hole,
Louisiana for seven weeks.

This should provide ample time for
visitors to pay final respects.

I'm sure some folks will want to
visit on a daily basis, such as my
mailman and that neighbor to
whom I still owe $20.

The flag outside of my local
Chucky Cheese shall be flown at
half mast, and my restraining order
should be temporarily suspended.

Upon eviction from my Hooker Hole estate, my remains are to be flown first class to London – via Las Vegas, where one final penny shall be dropped from the sky into a large slot machine that will win me absolutely nothing.

During the flight to London, gorgeous fight attendants/ Hawaiian Tropic models are to recite the safety information in Pig Latin, give away free booze, and check on the happiness of my coffin every 10 minutes.

Once we land in London,
my body shall be taken to
Westminster Synagogue on
a Shetland pony-driven carriage
past dozens of well-wishers,
reporters, and British people.

The ceremony is to be attended
by various heads of state:

- A Duchess from Paraguay;
- A Knight from the Round Table;
- Hamlet (or any Danish prince);
- Two guys from Germany
    wearing Lederhosen;
- Snow White;
- A Leprechaun; and
- Lou Ferrigno.

My bronze casket shall lie on
Persian carpeting, with Godiva
chocolates sprinkled around it.

Some of those Pecan Caramel
Duets would be nice, you know...
if you loved me.

My 1994 Jacksonville county
chili cook-off "participant" trophy
is to be retrieved from its Swiss
bank account and displayed next
to my rotting toenails.
(hint: secret ingredient).

The benediction shall be administered by that guy who played the Rabbi on *Seinfeld*.

If the Chancellor of Oxford University wants to award me a posthumous degree in molecular biology, I'm sure nobody in attendance will complain.

The audience shall then be treated to *I Saw the Sign*, by Ace of Base.

Next... a brief, 90-minute video clip of my life—the way I would like it to be remembered—shall be presented.

It will star Zac Efron, playing myself, and Megan Fox, playing the woman I deliver a pizza to.

My Uncle Larry is to then deliver
a touching, 45-second eulogy...
Followed by a half-hour tale of how
he once caught a 7-pound flounder
off the coast of Jones Beach.

The audience shall then be treated
to *I Saw the Sign*, by Ace of Base,
for a second time.

For the next four hours, friends
and family are to come up to
the altar and pay me a bunch of
compliments. All must howl to the
heavens that it should have been
them who died in the Ferris wheel
accident, not me.

After this, I would like the mayor
of Denver to present my casket
with a key to the city; no matter
that I never lived or visited there,
and openly gambled against the
Broncos at every opportunity.

My parents must get a member
of the Nobel Prize nominating
committee on speaker-phone
and ask if I will win this year.

If the committee person says no,
my parents are then to ask him/her
"Are you sure?"

If the answer is still no
(unlikely, but still), other
grieving participants are to
inquire on my behalf.

In the absurd, **million-to-one**
instance that I have still not been
bestowed the honor, everyone
must continue to call using different
fake Eastern-European accents.

Harry Potter shall then pass
around a collection plate for
my future shrine.

I expect this will lead to some sort
of internet campaign that will
be able to solicit donations from
distant lands far away, such as
Peru, Indonesia, and Atlantis.

The audience shall then, for a
third and final time, be treated to
I Saw the Sign, by Ace of Base.

My good friend, Brian, shall tattoo a
likeness of my face on everyone's
left butt cheek.

Finally, the doors to Westminster
Synagogue are to be unlocked,
allowing the audience to escape
(I mean, tearfully leave), vowing
to keep my memory alive...

After they find and kill Ace of Base.

DISPOSING OF MY CORPSE

After my funeral has finished being streamed via C-SPAN around the globe, my casket shall be carefully removed by the Manchester United fan club and handed to my parents like a delicious, unproportionally-large Sicilian pizza pie that just came out of the oven.

My parents must then carry my
casket on their backs for nine
months, thus completing the cycle
of life, and figuratively returning me
to my mother's womb.

Upon completion of their journey,
they should reach a forest that
is densely populated with many
rare trees, several small species
teetering on the verge of extinction,
and asbestos.

There, my body shall be cremated;
thus allowed to burn for days on
end. I'm sure nobody will mind.

Once I have been returned to ash,
my remains are to be divided into
four large, bedazzled Fabergé
eggs, handcrafted specifically
for this gloomy occasion by tiny
Russian elves.

Each of these eggs is to be
presented to a woman from my
past whom I loved deeply:

• Jennifer Schneider
    from Bayonne, NJ;
• Melissa Rothstein
    from Allentown, PA;
• Susan Chang
    from Syosset, NY; and
• Pamela Anderson
    from my DVD player.

Jennifer is to stop pretending she
always has a headache, Melissa is to
learn how to take a compliment,
and Susan is to divorce my cousin.

(Pamela, just stay awesome.)

The ladies are each commanded
to feed my ashes to a pet goldfish,
which shall be treated like royalty.

Each goldfish is to live in its
own 20-gallon tank decorated
with miniature Titanic replicas,
Ferris wheels, bonsai trees,
and Little Mermaid posters.

The goldfish shall be kept on a strictly
vegan diet (like Ted Danson).

When each goldfish eventually
passes away peacefully in its
sleep, the former love of my life
is hereby instructed to swallow
that goldfish whole and chase
it down with an entire bottle of
Boones Farm Snow Creek Berry.

The goldfish is to be digested to a
soothing Michael Bublé soundtrack
and its remains used as fertilizer
for a baby oak tree that she will
plant in her backyard.

Once the oak tree is large enough,
my ex-ball and chain is instructed
to carve my likeness into the tree
with one of those little screwdrivers
found in eyeglass repair kits.

In front of this tree that bears my
image, she will baptize her first
born son in my name.

In case she does not have a son,
I have left some of my sperm in a
safe deposit box at her local bank.

It's in the box that's titled:
"Future Ruler of Pandora".

The offspring will be required
to pay annual visits to my shrine.

The dates of each visit shall be flexible.

After all, I wouldn't want them to
go to any trouble on my behalf.

MY EARTHLY POSSESSIONS

I hereby bequeath all of my cash, stocks, bonds, savings, jewlery, and stolen credit card numbers to Prince Koffi Okoye of Nigeria.

I didn't read the fine print too carefully, but apparently he's going to turn my life's savings into millions for all of you!

I hereby bequeath my house back to the bank who loaned it to me back in 2007, for a down payment of $35 and a box of Goobers.

Wait… they already took it?
Great! Those guys must be
clairvoyant or something.

I hereby bequeath all of my debt to the Salvation Army. They really know how to raise a lot of funds; I'm sure they'll have all of my creditors paid in no time.

I hereby bequeath my iPhone to the 3 year-old Chinese kid who made it in the first place.

I hereby bequeath my 1996 Ford
Escort to my nephew, Aaron, who
will find that pushing it up hills
is a great way to bulk up for the
football team.

I hereby bequeath my
"honorable mention" winning
science fair project of the
Solar System to my cousin, Frank,
who's currently repeating
the 5th grade for the 5th time.

I hereby bequeath my VCR
collection to my Uncle Larry,
who still believes that DVD's
are "just a fad".

I hereby bequeath my broken
golf clubs to my Aunt Sally,
who suffers from terrible scoliosis.

I hereby bequeath my green
bananas to my grandmother.
(Unfortunately, this means that she
will now have to adjust her will, too.)

I hereby bequeath my Twinkies in
the cupboard to my great, great,
great, great, great grandchild.

I hereby bequeath my can of
Spam to his/her child.

I hereby bequeath my bed to
my cute upstairs neighbor, Sara,
who unfortunately never discovered
how comfy and supportive it is
while I was still alive.

I hereby bequeath my couch
to my good friend, Brian, who is
likely going to piss off his wife any
moment now.

I hereby bequeath my box
of matches to my good friend
Brian's son, Paul, who likes to
play "dragon" when his parents
are out of the house. I have no
idea what kind of game "dragon"
is, but I'm pretty sure it's harmless.

I hereby bequeath my bottle of
Smirnoff vodka in the freezer to
my friend, Nicole; she's a florist,
and the vodka can be used to help
keep her flowers nice and fresh.
She's also a drunk.

I hereby bequeath my naked
photos of my ex-girlfriend, Susan,
to my ex-girlfriend, Susan.

It's the only right thing to do.

First, someone will have to get
them back from the internet,
but that shouldn't be too difficult.

I hereby bequeath my leftover
Vicodin from 2003 to my buddy,
Dan, who's not very picky.

I hereby bequeath my skateboard
to my friend, Heather.

You may have trouble finding
my skateboard, because I don't
exactly own one. Somebody will
need to buy Heather a skateboard,
because I've already promised it to
her (over my dead body).

Tell her it's from me.
I'll owe you one.

I hereby bequeath my precious
"World's Greatest Son" coffee mug
to Oedipus, who also receives
my "World's Greatest Father" and
"World's Greatest Husband" mugs.

I hereby bequeath my sweaters to
Vanilla Ice, because he's ice cold...
And possibly homeless.

I hereby bequeath my piano
keyboard tie to Harry Connick, Jr.,
because he is literally the <u>only</u> guy
on the planet who can wear that
necktie and still get laid.

I hereby bequeath my Supercuts
loyalty card to Robert Pattinson,
so that he can finally get himself
a decent haircut.

I hereby bequeath my belt to
Jessica Rabbit, who has been
a very naughty girl.

I hereby bequeath my Debbie
Gibson *Out of the Blue* and
Electric Youth 8-tracks to
Debbie Gibson, because nobody
likes to hear Debbie Gibson sing
more than Debbie Gibson.

I hereby bequeath my gold chain
to celebrity hypnotist Kevin Stone,
who is getting very, very sleepy...

I hereby bequeath my thermometer
to Kate Upton, who is so hot she's
feverish. I'm also bequeathing
Kate some rubbing alcohol,
because she doesn't know where
that thermometer has been.

I hereby bequeath my unused
vacation days to Ferris Bueller;
he'll know what to do with them.

I hereby bequeath my Bible to
the Westboro Baptist Church.
Apparently, theirs are filled with a
bunch of misprints and typos.

I hereby bequeath my cracked
pipe to that drug addict who hangs
around in front of the all-night
bodega on the corner.
He's going to be so excited,
thinking you said "crack" pipe.
Make sure you wait a few minutes
before you inform him that he
heard you wrong. Laugh as hard
as you want; he'll forget all about
this later when he's high.

I hereby bequeath my elliptical
machine to the courteous spiders
who have been patiently watching
over it for the past six years.

I hereby bequeath my socks to the
Williamsburg Sock Puppet Festival,
with the condition that my socks
only play the lead roles, because
my socks are going to be stars.

I hereby bequeath my kilt to the
Scotsman whom I stole it from
when he was sleeping in an alley
back in 2004; no hard feelings.

I hereby bequeath my season tickets for the New York Islanders to our local EMT workers, who are used to being on the scene of unspeakable tragedies.

I hereby bequeath my fantasy football championship trophies from 2005 and 2008 to Kingbird Farms in Berkshire, New York. Thanks to me, they won't have to worry about any of their chickens escaping, because these trophies are literally chick magnets!

I hereby bequeath my teapot to anyone who is short and stout.

I hereby bequeath my flip flops
to my local Congressman.
(This one's just too easy.)

I hereby bequeath my mirror to
whoever is the fairest of them all.

I hereby bequeath my large
collection of Victoria Secret
catalogs to anyone who can
appreciate a good sale.

I hereby bequeath my subscription
to *Scientific American* magazine to
anyone with insomnia.

I hereby bequeath my microwave
to anyone who thinks that food
has too many nutrients.

I hereby bequeath my retro
Jimmy Buffett lunchbox to
anyone who's hankering for
a cheeseburger in paradise.

I hereby bequeath my Cuban
cigars to anyone who would like
a little extra cancer in their life.

I hereby bequeath my wok to
anyone who has some extra
storage space under their sink.

I hereby bequeath my dog
to anyone who likes to put
peanut butter on their balls.
Trust me on this.

I hereby bequeath my candlestick
to anyone who's looking to kill
Colonel Mustard in the library.

I hereby bequeath my underwear
to anyone who wishes they had
gotten to know me better.

I hereby bequeath my horse
tranquilizer to anyone who
wants a horse, but can't afford one.

SITTING SHIVA

My family, friends, co-workers,
bowling teammates, and online
chat-room pen pals must observe
a "week from hell" in my memory.

Every day shall start with
a wake-up song by Kathy Griffin,
and end with calculus homework.

Each night you are to buy a present that I would have appreciated, and then smash it over your heads.

You shall cover your mirrors with pictures of that *Playgirl* spread I did in college, so that I remain fresh (and air-brushed) in your minds.

You are not allowed to brush your teeth. This will be easier for some (ie: Uncle Larry) than others.

Every day shall be Monday.
When people ask you how you
enjoyed your weekend, you are
to reply that it sucked.

For the entire week, you are
to keep your iPod tuned to
Ke$ha's Pandora station.

Shave your eyebrows.

It will allow the tears to flow easier,
in case you find yourself crying
while upside-down.

You are only allowed to watch
movies that prominently feature
Pauly Shore.

You are to lay down under wooden
chairs, and then invite others to
sit in those wooden chairs.

No bitching about pain.

I'm fucking dead!

Nobody gives a shit about your
cracked ribs and punctured lung.

Your *emotional* pain over my loss,
however, is tragic.

Punch a total stranger in the face.
You'll feel better.

For breakfast and lunch you are
to eat only a mouthful of sawdust.

For dinner you may choose
between Hot Pockets or
another mouthful of sawdust.

At least you know what the
sawdust is made of.

You are not allowed to bathe.

An exception shall be made for
my ex-girlfriend, Jennifer, and
my cute upstairs neighbor, Sara.
Both should continue to bathe
constantly... together.

Is Sara really going along with this?
Why couldn't I think of this when I
was still alive?

Great...
Now Gandhi's laughing at me.

For the entire week, you must
root for the Milwaukee Bucks.

You are only allowed to drink Zima.

You are not allowed to sleep.
Every time you close your eyes,
someone is to stab you in the ribs.

MY SHRINE

Sitting atop Mount Olympus,
a beautiful temple shall be built in
the shape of a giant Snapple bottle,
reaching up towards the heavens.

Pilgrims shall be greeted by
a hologram of Alvin and the
Chipmunks, who will welcome
my visitors in three-part harmony.

Pilgrims shall remove all of their
clothing at the door, and then
pass by a large portrait of me
pointing and snickering at you.

There shall be a small stage
next to my portrait, where pilgrims
shall mime their favorite episodes
of *Night Court* and *Moesha* for
my viewing pleasure.

There are to be large purification tureens to catch your tears if you feel like crying.

If you do not feel like crying, miniature Buddhist monks will be on hand to kick you in the groin.

Each pilgrim shall bring one
Swedish Fish to sacrifice in
my honor.

There shall be no talking inside
of my shrine... the better to
hear looping recordings of my
nails scraping against a giant
chalkboard.

In the center of the room there
is to be a large sand pit.

Pilgrims will have the opportunity
to dig up miniature replicas of my
bones with tiny rakes, and then
put my body back together.

The first thing my realigned
skeleton would like is a
turkey sandwich.

In the corner, pilgrims should feel free to listen to my Uncle Larry lecturing about the benefits of investing in Swarovski crystals, as opposed to scams...

Such as buying stock in "worthless startups like Google."

There is to be a large reflecting pool. At the bottom of this pool shall lie 75 pennies. Taped to the side of the pool shall be a Kit Kat candy bar, which I will buy with my newfound 75 cents, and which I would like to save for later.

If it's not too much trouble,
a nearby volcano should
erupt every few years.

Pilgrims may search for years to find an old, ancient chalice which they may then use to drink from the reflecting pool...

Granting them absolutely nothing.

MY VIEW FROM HEAVEN

As I look down on all of you from my deluxe cloud in the sky, my eyes have been opened to many things which I could not see before my tragic demise:

There's a guy on a blind date in Toledo, OH who is wearing an awfully cheap toupee.

You would be surprised at how much butter this French chef uses in all of his sauces.

If the owner of a cherry red, 2009 Ford Focus hybrid in Kansas City, MO is currently reading this...

Your car is being towed.

There are two adorable squirrels fighting over a nut in a park in Albany, NY.

Is anyone else seeing this?

They're really going at it.

Someone should post this on YouTube.

So that's how they make doughnuts... ew... glad I didn't know that while I was alive.

This rookie gondola rower in Venice thinks he's such a good singer, but I've heard better.

That bee is pollinating the shit out of those flowers.

You really don't want to know how the ladies' restroom at McDonald's on Wilshire Blvd in Los Angeles came to look like that.

Trust me.

You are sooooo close to finding Amelia Earhart.

A high school football coach in Gary, IN is really letting his players hear it at halftime, although I wonder how he knows what exactly vaginas act like on a football field.

I can see my parents "doing it".

Honestly, it's really not as bad as I thought it would be.

Especially compared to what I saw in that ladies' restroom at McDonald's.

That painting of dogs playing poker above your mantle is off by about a quarter-inch to the left.

It's also really, really tacky.

But don't get me wrong.

I love it.

Mostly, though, I've been observing
these people who lounge around by
the beach in Ibiza, Spain.

There is such a tranquil sense of
comfort and joy, a true sense of
peace and freedom that I'm not
sure I ever truly experienced
during my time on earth.

People are smiling and kind,
and everyone radiates love
towards one another.

It's my reminder of the beautiful
world we all share with one
another.....

And everyone's topless.